THE HEART FEELS FIRST

THE HEART FEELS FIRST

A STORY OF REVIVAL AND RECOVERY

NAESHA PARKS

Tandem Light Press

Tandem Light Press

Tandem Light Press
950 Herrington Rd.
Suite C128
Lawrenceville, GA 30044

Copyright © 2014 by Naesha Parks

All rights reserved. No part of this book may be reproduced, scanned, or transmitted in any printed, electronic, mechanical, including photocopying, recording, or any information storage and retrieval system, without permission in writing from the publisher. Please do not participate in or encourage piracy of copyrighted materials in violation of the author's rights.

Tandem Light Press paperback edition July 2014

ISBN: 978-0-9854437-5-7

Library of Congress Control Number: 2014949236

Biblical passages are from the King James Bible

Printed in the United States of America

I would like to dedicate this book to my children: Chandler, Sydney, Chance, and Reese. I am so proud to be your mother. Let the light that shines within us draw others closer to the presence of God.

"... the sufferings of this present time are not worthy to be compared with the glory which shall be revealed in us."

Romans 8:18

TABLE OF CONTENTS

Acknowledgments	xi
Introduction	xv
I	1
II	18
III	57
IV	74
About the Author	89

ACKNOWLEDGMENTS

I WOULD LIKE to thank God for allowing me to be a living example of what it means to be a miracle. A huge thank you also to the following people …

To Dr. Pamela Larde for giving me the opportunity to share my story with the world.

To Caroline Donahue for always challenging me to dig deeper so that I could uncover the hidden treasure in my story.

To my husband, Keenan, for being mom and dad when I couldn't be. I love you KJ.

To Apostle McCoy for allowing God to speak through him regarding the secret things in my life and for being my father in Christ.

I would like to thank my pastors Michael and Bernita Mitchell for teaching me how to understand my purpose and recognize my destiny. You helped me to pick up the pieces of my life and discover my rightful place in God.

To Roscoe and Ann Perry for allowing me to borrow their most precious gift "Christina." I could not have made it without your family. Christina, He that has begun a great work in you is able to perfect it. Thank you "Stina."

I would like to thank Eddie Curry and Katie Hunt for standing still in the middle of the storm and supporting me throughout my recovery. Daddy, you are an amazing man.

To George and Apryl Burgess for being my pillar of support. George, you both are perfect examples of what it means to be strong.

Thank you to Yvette Foster for allowing God to use you to save my life by making the 911 call. I will always love and be grateful to you for hearing me that day at McDonalds.

To Skylar and Courtney Burgess for being the best little sister and brother that any person could ask for.

To Joyce and April Cox for the nights you rocked my little man to sleep when I couldn't.

To Wendy Lanham and Donovia Culbreath for supporting others in their efforts to support me. Your presence truly made a difference.

To Herman and Nancy Smith for being my rock throughout my journey.

To Tavories and Naeconda Ivey for standing firm and believing in our God, who is a healer.

To Brian Smith for being present throughout my journey and believing in my recovery.

To my Evans Elementary family, who carried me when I was unable to stand alone.

To LeAnne Gregg for encouraging and supporting me.

To Deborah Williams for your ability to bring calmness to every situation and reminding me to focus on all that is good.

To Keith Brown for giving me the first one dollar bill towards writing my first book.

To Elder Daniels and his wife for ushering in the presence of God in a time that my family needed it the most.

To Preston and Wanda Sunket for your unwavering support.

To Grandma Carolyn Johnson for standing with me and my family when things did not look so good.

To Mary Frances Reese "Granny' for leading me on the path where I received the only perfect gift in my life, Jesus Christ.

To Joe and Carmen Williams for helping my family to remember that God is always in control even when things appeared to be spinning out of control.

To Dr. Vinayak Kamath and Lyndi Baldy for their medical expertise and friendship over the years.

To Dr. Andrew Mac Bowman for taking over a dark situation and allowing God to use you to bring in the light.

I want to thank Anne Marie for her help with all the marketing of my book.

Yuvondrea Tremble and Tonia Ellis for reminding me that you don't have to share the same DNA to be related. Also, a great big thank you to Judy Holton for her close attention to details.

INTRODUCTION

Woman's recovery turns out to be more rare than disease

The Augusta Chronicle

By **Tom Corwin**| *Staff Writer*
Monday, November 17, 2008

Naesha Parks believes it was divine inspiration that led her to take her sudden bad feeling more seriously and urge a friend to call 911.

She suddenly remembered a friend she hadn't spoken to in years describing his first heart attack.

"The last thing that I remember was saying to her, 'I can't die. Who's going to care for my children?'" said Mrs. Parks, 35. "And I woke up a week-and-a-half later in Open Heart Recovery."

That she was able to wake up at all stumps even her heart surgeon.

What felled Mrs. Parks was an extremely rare and deadly condition called spontaneous coronary artery dissection. There have been only about 300 documented cases, although there have probably been more that were not written up, said Mazullah Kamran, assistant professor of medicine at Mount Sinai School of Medicine and co-author of a review article on the disease last month in The Journal of Interventional Cardiology.

"It's probably an underestimate because most of the people just don't make it out of the hospital or don't get a definitive test," he said.

For reasons that are still unclear, the coronary arteries split open and about 20 percent of patients die, although improved imaging and advanced treatment have raised survival rates, Dr. Kamran said.

It most often strikes in younger women before or after they give birth, as it did with Mrs. Parks, and may be triggered by hormone levels, but there is no definitive cause and only hypotheses at this point, he said.

She had just had a son, Reese, nine days before, in June, and a friend was taking her out to get a soda because she was tired of being cooped up in the house.

"All of a sudden, I started to feel really bad, an indescribable feeling," she said. "I can't say my heart was hurting a whole lot. I just felt bad."

She remembered her friend's description of the heart attack and knew what she was feeling could be a sign of something more serious, so she got her friend to call an ambulance.

It was a pulmonary embolism, a clot caught in her lungs, that knocked her down at first. But after a couple of days of treatment at University Hospital, she began to show signs of heart trouble. A cardiac catheterization came up with some shocking results. One of the three main arteries feeding blood to her heart was "extremely small," and the other two had completely split, said her cardiothoracic surgeon, M. Vinayak Kamath.

"Basically, there was no amount (of blood) going through" to the heart muscle, he said. As they were trying to get her into surgery, her heart stopped and it took 20-25 minutes to revive her and get her on a heart-lung bypass machine. Dr. Kamath did three coronary artery bypass grafts, but he was not optimistic.

"She was dead, basically," he said. "This was as close to dead as I have seen before."

But slowly, hour by hour, Mrs. Parks seemed to improve. Dr. Kamath left her chest cavity open and started calling around to see if he could get her a heart transplant. Medical College of Georgia

Hospital couldn't help him, and the University of Alabama-Birmingham couldn't take her in her condition. The next day, out of the blue, two top heart programs — the Cleveland Clinic and Massachusetts General Hospital — called offering a plane to bring her in, having heard about her story, Dr. Kamath said.

Still, he hesitated to move her. And his faith was rewarded in improvements "almost on an hourly basis," he said. After spending two nights by her bedside, afraid she might suddenly take a turn for the worse, Dr. Kamath finally closed her chest. And she began the long road to recovery.

"There's no way scientifically to explain her recovery," said Dr. Kamath. "In her case, it was just nothing short of a miracle. I feel sort of humbled."

It is not a mystery to Mrs. Parks. Family, friends, strangers in churches as far away as Germany added her to their prayers. And it is faith that made the difference, she believes.

"If I were not a believer in miracles myself, there would have been a strong possibility that I might not have received one," she said. "I think that when man says no, it's the perfect opportunity for God to say yes. And that is exactly what happened."

I

"To unto whomsoever much is given, of him shall be much required."

Luke 12:48

WHO WOULD HAVE ever thought that after all the life lessons and teachable moments I've experienced, that all of my hopes and dreams would be reduced to nothing after sixteen minutes?

My life growing up was pretty uneventful. As a child, I grew up with my grandmother in Thomson, Georgia—a small rural town where everyone knew each other by name. I lived with them until late middle school when I went to live with my mother. My grandmother raised me to be a God-fearing woman, much like the way she was raised. My grandfather was quite the opposite; as many would say, "God was still working on him." He was a good man who stood on what he believed in. He loved his family and was known by everyone in town.

When I was ten, my mother had a second child. My beautiful little sister had dark skin, beautiful brown eyes, and a head full of black hair. Because of our age difference, I spent quite a bit of time helping to take care of her. I had high hopes for her too. I loved her as if she were my own.

As soon as I was able to work, I applied for and was hired as a cashier at a McDonald's not far from home. I quickly learned that what my mother was doing was not easy. I was able to juggle school and work while helping take care of my sister. I often asked myself how I made it. Looking back, it could have only been through God's grace. I continued to work part-time while attending high school. My days consisted of school, work, and worship.

After high school, I made excuses as to why I couldn't go right to college. I convinced myself that I couldn't do it and that there were no financial resources available to me. Oh, if there was an excuse, I researched and used it. So, for about a year, I worked full time. It wasn't until I approached my second year of not continuing my education that I had a very candid conversation with my godmother about what it was going to take for me to be the person I was called to be. As well as telling me to get off of my rear end, she helped me realize that *I* had to be the one to take the initiative to change my circumstances. She frankly reminded me that the world was waiting on me to take control and pursue my dream of being successful in life. The light bulb went on! I decided then that it was time for me to begin my journey and register for college.

Along the way, I fell in love. I was smitten. I fell hard, too. My whole world centered around one person. Out of a seven-year relationship, my beautiful daughter, Sydney was conceived. I remember the day she was born. She was very small: six pounds and eight ounces with a light complexion and a head full of hair. So tiny and innocent. I looked at her and knew that I had never really known what love was. I can still smell that new baby scent in my nostrils.

Having Sydney forced me to remain focused, knowing that her life was in my hands. I worked my way through school part-time. Initially, I attended Georgia Military College. The years I spent there were years of growing pains. Georgia Military College was on a military base. I went to school at night, so I was always a little nervous when I left campus. I worked hard to find balance between family, working all day, and school at night. Eventually, my perseverance paid off. I graduated from Georgia Military College with honors!

I made it a practice to go to bed and wake up talking to God. After many nights of praying and asking God what I was being called to do, I made the commitment to become a teacher. Without doubting myself or listening to any naysayers, I knew. I was born to teach. Now, I was able to fast forward into the next stage of my life, which would lead to my career as an educator.

I applied for and was accepted into a well-known accredited school, Augusta State University. The college campus was much bigger than Georgia Military. I was so taken aback by the size of the campus, large student body and everything that made the campus unique. As a student at Augusta State, I began to intentionally embrace becoming a teacher. Everything I did at the university was done with great pride. As I took courses, I slowly began to realize the impact I could potentially have on young lives. Wow! What a powerful realization to come to. There was no room for me to make a mistake. I went through my courses without any major setbacks. I graduated from the university with all the tools I needed to teach like a champion! That was exactly what I did. I spent endless nights planning exciting lessons for my students. Aside from my daughter, I lived to make them happy.

I didn't think life could get any better; quite the opposite though. I was soon scheduling my daughter for a literacy program! I called the office and a gentleman answered. His voice was strong and he spoke with confidence. To me, confidence is always an attractive quality in a man. His name was Keenan. We scheduled my daughter's tutoring session. Somehow, we got on the topic of life, our kids and our families, hopes, dreams, ambitions and our spiritual walk. It was a very intense conversation. He offered me free circus tickets. I was so intrigued by him that I got all dolled up and went to pick them up the very next day.

Can you believe that he acted as if he didn't notice me at all? I was hurt! Then, the phone rang. In my mind, I was thinking of the many things he could have wanted. Did he want to talk to me about the next sessions? Tell me there was something wrong with the tickets? Everything crossed my mind before I answered the phone. It was none of those things. He wanted to ask me out on a date. Our relationship moved quickly, and I was married and pregnant again before I knew it.

After teaching for a couple of years, I pursued a doctoral program. During this program, I would learn the power of perseverance and faith. This program was designed for individuals who worked and had a passionate drive to go further in their career. Well, that described me perfectly, so I enrolled. I worked during the week and took classes on the weekend. The doctoral class required one year of course work and then writing your dissertation.

I can explicitly recall my last day with my peers. I was nine months pregnant. We made plans to collaborate and graduate together. Our goodbyes were full of emotion and in the upcoming year, we all would feel the loneliness of not seeing one another every Saturday and Sunday again. None of us had any idea that the next call they would receive about me would be one asking them to pray because there was only a slight chance I would live.

A monumental milestone was giving birth to my handsome young man, Reese, who would forever change my world. It was dark, early morning on June 12th. I had a cesarean so everything was planned and we were ready to go. I had an uneventful surgery and was able to go home after three days in the hospital. On the third day at 8:00 a.m., my bags were filled with prescriptions, doctors' orders, and brochures on how to take care of the baby. I was packed, wheelchair-bound, and ready to go. I hated the wheelchair, but the hospital rules were that all patients had to be in a wheelchair when they left the hospital.

My husband and I arrived home. Our house was loaded with gifts for our son. There were diapers, formula, toys, Bumbos, and all sorts of things that people bought within the three days I was in the hospital. We could barely get through the door. My husband had spent most of his time at the hospital so he didn't have time to sort through and move the gifts. We didn't have an official nursery set up in the extra bedroom. My son had a wooden portable crib in our bedroom. I planned to keep my sweet little boy near me at all times. Plus, I didn't want to have to walk any further than my bed when I got up three or four times during the night. Having a newborn was going to make us bald before it was all over with.

My husband and I were home together because he was

on leave from his job. He worked as a purchasing agent out of town in Warner Robins. He was normally home on the weekends. To be honest, I wasn't used to having him home all the time. So, as a result, I found myself needing to take a breather.

Suddenly, I was beginning to get what many people refer to as cabin fever. I asked one of my closest friends to come and take me to McDonald's to have a diet coke. The McDonald's was located off of a busy street. It was in the heat of the summer so the restaurant was packed with children and their parents along with workers taking their lunch break. It was a busy day for the McDonald's staff.

My friend and I sat in the enclosed area closest to the playground and of course, near the bathrooms. We conversed, talked about losing weight and me having a new baby. We were joking that I was starting all over since my daughter was ten years old. It didn't take long for me to start missing my little man. My timing was perfect because both of us ordered a large diet coke and we were both about finished. I was packing up to go and suddenly, I started to feel bad. The pain was not like any pain that I had felt. It felt as though someone had their fist in the center of my chest and a mental black cloud of despair came over me. I looked at my friend who was gazing at her new blackberry phone. Before I could speak, she asked, "Hey, before you go home, we should go by Best Buy and get new cell phone cases."

I looked at her and said, "I don't feel good, would you take me home?" She of course said yes. I told her that I needed to use the bathroom first. I went into the restroom and walked into the stall. I used the restroom and I remember looking at the blue colored stalls thinking, I just need to go home and get in the bed. I thought a few hours of sleep might make things better and I would be fine. After I finished in the restroom, I walked over to the sink. I remember that walk as being one of the longest most strenuous walks I had ever taken. Once I left the bathroom and got to the sink. I felt as though I had run a marathon. I washed my hands and looked in the mirror. I noticed that I was sweating like nothing that I had experienced before. I don't sweat often, but big beads of it were pouring down my face. A feeling of doom washed over me. I was terrified.

As I stepped out of the bathroom and into the lunchtime rush, where people were talking, laughing and enjoying their meals, something surreal occurred. I felt as though my spirit left my body and went back to the home of two of my longtime friends, Joe and Diana. Joe had a very keen sense of humor. We always referred to him as "the clock that just kept ticking." This particular day, Joe was describing his first heart attack. He was sitting in his recliner moving his foot in a fast motion. He looked at me and said, "Naesha, when I had my first heart attack, it felt like an elephant was sitting on my chest."

The vision was so real. I couldn't understand what was happening. I was supposed to be at McDonald's having a diet coke but instead I was in their living room. I had not spoken to my friends in over five years. However, that was the last conversation we had with one another. Seconds later, I was back at McDonalds. Still hurting and still in pain, once I gathered my thoughts, I realized that God would not have taken me back to that specific conversation if there wasn't something He wanted me to know. I felt it was God's intervention on my behalf. If He had not allowed me to have a two-minute out-of-body experience, I may have gone home and gone to bed. I believe I would have never awakened. At that moment, I acknowledged that God was trying to tell me something, so I listened.

I walked over to my friend, still sweating, feeling calm despite the pain in my chest. I looked at her and quietly said, "I want you to listen to me very carefully: I am very sick."

She responded, "I'll go and get the car."

"No, you don't understand. I am very sick and you have to call 911." I sat down in the chair. At the time, I was wearing a dress but I had on a waist belt. Without considering my surroundings, I pulled up my dress and ripped off the waist belt. The man who sat at the table across from us got a little more than lunch that day. He got a close-up view of everything that was under my dress—and I do mean *everything*. I looked at my friend's hand and she was shaking as if she was being overtaken by fear. "Did you call?" I asked.

"Yes, I called."

"Call them again." Over and over again, I asked. I know now that she pretended to dial the number again because she didn't want to upset me. I looked at her and said, "I can't die; who will take care of my kids?"

* * *

It was a beautiful day outside. I was off work and taking the kids to the movies. I received a call from Yvette—she was at McDonald's on Davis Road, and she said that Naesha was sick; she had called 911.

I arrived at McDonald's the same time as the EMT's. When they asked me where to take her, I told them if she was in immediate danger to take her to the closest hospital; if not, take her to University. I met them at University ER. She had calmed down some and they had started running some tests. From the tests they were running, I knew they were thinking she had an embolism. She was admitted soon after.

I stayed with Naesha until her mom arrived, and left to pick up the kids from Yvette. Since Naesha was still not feeling well a day or so later, they decided to do a cardiac cath[eter]. I was at work and had called down to the hospital to check on her. Her sister told me they were taking her to the cath lab. I immediately left work and headed for the hospital.

When I arrived, I saw her sister. She was scared and upset, and she told me they were taking Naesha to surgery. We were told to wait in the waiting room. None of us were really sure what was going on. When we got there, Naesha's mom Nancy was there. We all hugged and assured each other that things were going to be okay. Then the nurse came in. She told us that Naesha's heart had stopped. I thought my heart stopped right along with hers. Nancy and I clung to each other, crying and praying at the same time. The nurse told us to calm down: they had been able to revive her, but she had been out for a while. She said that she would keep us informed.

– Apryl, Naesha's godmother

***

I know Naesha as my one and only big sister. I think my mom probably utilized her as an "in-home" and free babysitter, because I remember spending most of my childhood with her. I'm sure I got on her nerves. I know she probably wanted to be a regular teenager, and not have her little sister tag along everywhere with her, but she handled it well, and sort of adopted me as her first child.

A bit of background info before the rest of the

story: Naesha and I drifted apart when I moved with my grandmother. Although she took care of me still and was there for me when I needed her, during that time I felt like I had absolutely no one. We were not close then, and it just kind of carried on up until she had her son.

When I heard Naesha was going into the hospital, I was working at Earth Fare part-time. I was on my way to work when my mom called me. It was a Saturday, and I went to work and told my mom that I would come spend the night with them. The whole time, I had no idea that her condition was so serious, so I figured that next day we would probably all go home. *I am just going to go up here and sit and play games on my phone the whole time,* I thought to myself. *After all, we're not really all that close anyway. I don't see how my presence could make any difference.*

I remember going into her room and she smiled and said "Momma, she did come!" (I guess that was during a time in my life when I was not dependable. I should add that I was contemplating not going that day at work.) I was sure she would be fine. So during the night every time I would manage to fall asleep in that uncomfortable little chair, my sister would wake up in pain. I remember thinking, *she sure isn't getting better like the doctor said she would.*

We talked to him on Sunday morning. He said they

had something called a 64-slice CT that we would have to wait until Monday to be able to use, but if we really just wanted to make sure that nothing else was going on, he would do a cardiac catheterization. We jumped at it. He explained what a routine procedure it was, and the risks involved. I remember him distinctly saying, "I'm about 99.9% sure everything is fine, and there won't be any complications. This procedure is done all the time with no complications."

After about two and a half hours of waiting for this forty-five minute procedure to be done, her doctor came out. He was covered in blood. He held his head down as he softly said, "I don't know what happened. Every time we progressed the catheter, her artery just split." It didn't occur to us how serious this was until he said she would have to go into emergency surgery. He already had the doctor there who would do the surgery. We had just enough time to go and tell her that we loved her, and she looked over at my mom and said, "Is it a good doctor who is going to do the surgery?" My mom told her yes, naturally. We had no idea who her surgeon was, but we trusted in his ability because he told us that she would need a lot of prayer, and we knew then that he believed in God.

– Naeconda, Naesha's sister

***

My daughter and I, like many other moms and daughters, have had some issues in the past, but I can truly say that from that day until this day, I no longer remember them. They are truly insignificant.

I remember getting the call to come to the hospital. I don't even know who it was that called me. The next thing I remember was being at University Hospital from her bedside to the cardiac cath lab. I remember having to contain myself because of her husband. I didn't want anyone to see the ugly side of me, but before the cardiac cath, I thought to myself, just as mother's do, *Why can't I do something to get her out of this pain?* I remember wanting to bear it for her. The morphine did little to help. It was every ten minutes, seems like, and my daughter telling me, "Mama, something is wrong." How helpless. How defeated. How hopeless. But I had to keep it together. Finally, she was feeling so bad that I went out to the nurses' station and I said, "Damnit, somebody better do something!"

My mind takes me back now to a couple of weeks before Reese was born. Naesha was very short of breath and I went to a cardiologist with her—the one I would later have to fire, and he was very happy that I did release him and he told me so. But at this appointment, they did all the standard tests they could do and said it might be something hidden, like a murmur from birth. She was already considered high risk, but she was breathing very heavy. (The weight from the pregnancy was how I summed it up.) The doctor said he would follow this up after the pregnancy. That enemy Satan had his plan in place to kill my daughter.

So the doctor was called in because we had been so persistent with the nurses about calling him. This time, he said that her cardiac labs were a little off. They had decided to do a cath on Monday, but since her labs were off, they would do it today. These doctors were father and son and the younger one was on call. He called his father in to assist. The story began like this:

"We are going to go in and look for blockage and if there is any, we will do what they call a stent." (These terms I was very familiar with because of thirty-two years of experience in the medical field.)

He went on to say some of the things that could happen. To my inner-self, I was saying, "Shut up, and get her out of this pain!" I drifted off from him because she was in excruciating pain, looking like a little girl who needed her mom to fix this. I drifted back to the young, inexperienced doctor who'd gotten my attention: "There is a 90% chance of this not happening, it is a condition called coronary artery dissection, where the arteries will start to split. This is rare. It happens with pregnant women sometimes after childbirth because of the pregnancy hormones, but don't worry, we don't think it can happen to her."

I said, "Okay, go ahead with the procedure. How long will it take?"

About an hour is what I heard.

I remember it was raining outside. I remember it used to always rain when somebody died. I thought to myself, *I can't have my child die.* I never thought it could happen to me. Naturally, I begged God to let her make it. I had to pray. I went off to the bathroom, but I was always praying under my breath. By now, the world had stopped turning. Time stood still. It seems like at least a day had passed in my mind, but no more than two hours had gone by. I paced, cried, prayed. The doctors emerged. Both gowns bloody, very bloody, and the look they had—like two scared animals. Worse than that deer in the headlights look. I know that at that minute they wanted the floor to open up and swallow them.

And the young one said, "Remember what I told you can't happen? Well it did. Every time we tried to put the stent in, her arteries would just pull back. She needs to go to surgery right away. She had blockage." (To this day, I don't believe that.)

"Can I see her?" I asked. "Well, what are you waiting for? You have my permission, but let me see her."

I heard the words: "You have to make it quick."

By now they were bringing her out of the cath lab.

She was really sick looking. Again, I saw that little girl looking for mommy to fix it.

"Mama, who is my doctor?"

"The best on the planet."

I did not know the man; never met him. My daughter had asked me once before when I went to the ER with her when she had something totally unrelated to this (An ear infection, I think): "Am I going to die?" I told her no.

This time, she did not ask, but it was written all over her face. She didn't have to ask. Another breath, prayers, *God don't let her die.* I couldn't wait to be alone and pray to God. I didn't think I deserved to be heard by God, but that was not going to stop me. I turned to go to open heart recovery. The door closed behind me. I was headed to the bathroom to cry out to God, but I heard a voice: "Parks family?"

I turned to go to the open heart waiting area. "Yes?"

This small blonde white woman asked, "Are you her mother?"

"Yes, I am," I said.

"I am sorry to tell you your daughter died outside the operating room."

– Nancy, Naesha's mom

II

*"Every good and perfect gifts come from above,
and cometh down from the Father of lights."*

James 1:17

"I don't know what is going on, but it is certainly something serious bad," the cardiologist's voice came over the phone one afternoon in the summer of 2008. "I am taking this patient, Naesha Parks, to the cardiac cath lab. She came in with post-partum pulmonary embolus, five days out from a normal delivery, and she is going into cardiac shock.

Blood clots migrating to the mother's lungs after the baby is born is not unheard of, but why was her heart crumping?

By the time I got to the hospital, Mrs. Parks was

being wheeled out of the cath lab and the cardiologist was stabilizing her.

"You won't believe what I found," he said in an urgent whisper. "She has SCAD and I can't do anything about it. You will have to try something right away with open-heart surgery. Either way, I don't think she is going to make it. Good luck."

SCAD, short for Spontaneous Coronary Artery Dissection, is a very rare condition where the coronary artery, the tiny blood vessel that carries oxygen and blood into the heart muscle so that they can keep pumping, gets blocked by blood streaming in between the layers of the wall of the artery. Very few survivors have been reported because, with no blood reaching the heart muscle, it dies almost instantaneously. There were no survivors reported with the deadly combination of blood clots in the lung and SCAD.

I turned to examine Mrs. Parks. There she lay, fighting to breathe, terrified. Now crying, she grabbed my hand and said "Don't let me die, I have little ones to take care of."

Those were her last words as her eyes rolled back and her heart stopped.

The breathing tube went in immediately, and chest compressions began. The team was almost ready as we wheeled her into the operating room. We hastily moved her onto the OR table, and with the CPR going on, splashed some iodine on her chest and started her operation as the anesthesia drugs went into her system.

What we found was a heart seemingly beyond repair. All her coronary arteries were clogged from one end to the other with blood clots. There was no inside lining or "intima" left where we opened up the artery. The lining had been torn away.

With the patient now stable on the heart lung bypass machine, we spent a half hour sucking clots out of her coronary arteries and finally found three areas that I could plug in vein bypasses to reestablish blood and oxygen supply to the heart muscle.

– Dr. Kamath, Naesha's surgeon

***

It is a great honor and pleasure for me to give my thoughts and share my perspective on Naesha Parks, whom I consider both a friend and a patient. She and I have been together for several years now; long enough for me to trust what she says and feels about herself, so when she was convinced that something bad was going to happen during her pregnancy, I referred her to Dr. Ware, a specialist in maternal fetal medicine whom I trust and respect. I was very happy that her pregnancy went without a hitch and had forgotten about her fears. But when I received the call from her managing surgeon,

I realized her fears were not those of an anxious woman, but that she had been spot on with her intuition.

He had sent me his operative report in addition to contacting me. I was incredibly shocked to read a description of the events that transpired in the cath lab. He held her heart in his hand and when she reached up to him as she was dying she said, "Don't let me die, I have two children to raise," he took her at her word and refused to give up.

I came to visit Naesha in the ICU while she was in an induced coma, with her chest filleted open on an assist pump for her heart and I said to myself, "My God, how could this have happened?!"

– Dr. Sarah Speese, Naesha's OB/GYN

***

I found myself in a cold, bare room. My body felt heavy, as if I hadn't moved for a long time. I reached out to touch the wall nearest to me, but it seemed so far away. My attempts were unsuccessful. While stretching my hand, I was thinking that I had to find a way to confirm whether I was dreaming. I gazed around the room, thinking to myself, *Where am I and what did I do to be in such an isolated place?*

There were tall, brown cabinets that looked like the ones you might see in a hospital room. Just as I was thinking that I had found my answer, my eyes became fixated on the round standard, black clock that was on the wall directly across the room. I wondered to myself where time had gone. It was just around noon when I'd left home to have a Diet Coke at McDonald's. *Surely I'm dreaming,* I thought. *Why am I here and not in my bed?* Those were the questions that I wanted answered.

I was unable to move my head and body to get a full scope of the room. Out of the corner of my left eye, I could see what appeared to be a glass-enclosed office, but there was no one inside. I remember such a feeling of emptiness at the very same time that I noticed there was no one in the room. To the right of me was what seemed like a large amount of empty space. There was some sort of small machine mounted on the wall, but besides this machine, there was nothing around or near it to give me an idea what type of machine it was.

Then, the feeling of loneliness resurfaced. I was really alone. I became terrified, and a spirit of fear overshadowed me again. Suddenly, I had a strong desire to be near someone familiar. There were thoughts and questions racing through my mind: *Where is my husband, where is my mom, where are my kids, where am I and why am I here, why am I hooked up to this machine, what is this tube in my throat and chest,* and finally, *what did I do to deserve to be in this condition?*

My eyes were racing back and forth. I noticed that there was another cabinet directly in front of me. There was movement on top of it. Initially, I was unable to focus so that I could see where the movement was coming from. I squinted my eyes but was still unable to identify the source.

I looked to the right of the cabinet and noticed the clock again. It was about 5:16 in the morning. I remember the time clearly, because I started to wonder where I could possibly be at 5:16 in the morning. Who—or what—was up this early and what could they possibly be looking for up there? Just as I was trying to re-focus my vision, I was able to make out exactly what was moving on top of the cabinet.

It was a beautiful, small angel. Her skin was a very radiant, unique gold color. Realizing what I was seeing, I became unsettled in my spirit. I was scared. Had she come for me? Thoughts of death, life after death, my family, my children, and all of my hopes and dreams being prematurely terminated. This just could not happen now.

The angel approached my bedside; she was no taller than the average second grader. Her eyes were a deep, dark black. It was almost as if they were the window to many souls (not just mine). Her hair was the same radiating, gold color as her skin, and it appeared to be very rugged and coarse.

Even though I was terrified, I somehow managed to find my voice. I very boldly said to her "I can't go with you. What about my children?"

She responded in a low-pitched, calming voice, "I don't want you to worry; everything is going to be alright."

"You don't understand," I said. "I can't. Who will take care of my kids? They need me."

She repeated, "I don't want you to worry. Everything is going to be alright."

It was like a war of words. We both kept saying the same things. I felt a mixture of emotions as she spoke. There was a level of comfort accompanied by a strong feeling of anxiety. I thought of all the movies I had watched over the years. If an angel appeared, it usually meant that the person who saw her was getting ready to cross over.

***

Then came the long wait. The triple bypasses were working well and oxygen was now flowing into her heart muscle, but was it too late? Would the heart survive—*could* it survive?

Things were looking grim an hour later. We started preparations to place her on a long-term bypass machine, known as ECMO, to support her circulation and oxygenation. Calls were made to transplant centers around the country. Perhaps she could be a candidate for transplant. But the consensus was that she was too sick to be transferred and that she was not going to make it any way.

Finally, about five hours into her surgery, with the family mentally prepared for her demise, we began the preparation for ECMO support. Then, all of a sudden, the heart started flickering, then a beat, then a few minutes later another beat, and then, miracle of miracles, the heart started beating slowly and she had a heart rhythm!

But the heart was still too weak to pump on its own and it was too swollen for us to close her chest. So we transported her, fully under anesthesia and on the breathing machine, to the intensive care with her chest open and all the support devices in place to keep her circulation going.

It was a long wait but slowly and steadily, over the next few days, her heart became stronger. We could close her chest. We could slowly wake her up and about two weeks from her surgery, she came off the breathing machine and she could talk!

The support systems came out one by one as her heart became stronger and the clots in her lungs started dissolving. Six weeks from her surgery, Mrs. Naesha Parks walked out of the hospital to a happy and grateful waiting family.

– Dr. Kamath

***

In the initial hours post-surgery, her savior was frantically trying to find a facility that would accept her for a heart transplant. Neither MCG nor Emory would touch her. UAB was willing to take her, but she was too unstable for transport. We felt completely helpless. It was my role to comfort the family and pray; and to struggle to answer the unanswerable questions "WHY?!"

None of us understood why this was happening to our friend and family member. Here was this young, vivacious thirty-four-year-old woman, who was just two weeks after delivering a very healthy baby, now lying comatose near death.

Naesha's story is proof that miracles do happen, and that with God anything is possible! She started turning the corner as her heart function improved. The only question that remained was whether she would retain normal cognitive function after such an incredible ordeal of being resuscitated for forty-five minutes. Imagine my surprise and pleasure when I was able to sit down to talk to her in her hospital room and see that she was the same Naesha! She and I talked about the angel she saw on the shelf in front of her. At the time, I thought it was a narcotic-induced hallucination. However, I now believe that an angel may very well have been all that kept Naesha out of death's door.

– Sarah Speese

Meanwhile in the waiting room ...

Nancy was on her knees asking God to save her child, and I was asking Him why and refusing to accept the fact that he would take her from us. I don't know how much time passed before Dr. Kamath came in to talk us. I will never forget that moment. He said he had done all he could; now we just had to wait and pray. She was a very sick young woman.

Hours later, they let us go in to see her. I was amazed at all the medicines and machines that were plugged into her. And the look on the nurses faces ... well, it didn't give us more hope. Now the waiting began. Nancy and I never left that waiting room except to go in to see her. I remember that every little noise had me on my feet thinking it was someone with news.

One of the options they presented us with was to move her to Ohio for a heart transplant. I wanted them to do anything to make her better, but Keenen spoke the words of reason and said no: she needed her family with her. He was right.

– Apryl, godmother

***

I screamed and fell down to the floor. *It's my fault.*

Suddenly, this woman tells me they got her heart started again. When Dr. Kamath finally came, he told me that things did not look good, and we would need to say plenty of prayers. He also stated that all the stars were aligned correctly. I did not know what that meant, until I later found out he was not a Christian. I heard words like, she would need a new heart, and her chest would have to remain open. I never prayed so hard in my life. It was very constant begging of God.

Naesha's godmother, who is still my very best friend, was right there beside me. We became friends through a meeting/fight at work. We were both young—twenty-six, if that. After that, we became roommates. Apryl, if you are reading this, I will never forget that day. You promised me one night that you would take care of her if I couldn't and you have been there when I wasn't; you were true to your word.

The next thing I remember was a host of friends wanting to see her. Her godmother, sister, and I were not going to let that happen. See, we knew the *real* Naesha. She would never want anyone to see her at that point in her life, fighting for her very existence. She is particular about her looks; never a hair out of place. She invented the mani/pedi. So while I was standing guard at her room, a middle-aged lady with lots of moles on her face stood out. That, and the fact that was wearing all white.

She asked, "You are the mother?" I nodded my head. Then she said, "I was there when the man said, 'No!' I am always there when he does surgery, and he had not ever looked so confused ... that is when her heart stopped. I told him that if it is a spirit of confusion," she went on, "then it is not from God; so, he continued working on her."

She went on to say, "God has some amazing plans for your daughter; He intends to use her in a very special way. She is important to Him." Then she asked the question that everyone else got a no answer to: "Can I see her?"

I never answered. My heart said yes. My eyes were still fixed on her face, on the moles. My body moved to the side without any effort on my part. I walked up and down the hall for what seemed to be at least half an hour. I noticed that she was very close down in my daughter's face having a conversation, a long one. Due to the circumstances of what kind of shape my daughter was in, I didn't see how she could remember the conversation, but she said she does. This was a gift for me also because the lady was an angel. I had the pleasure of meeting her on her divine assignment. I am a very fortunate mother. That man said no, but Our Heavenly Father said yes.

– Nancy, mom

***

It seemed like we were only in the cardiac recovery waiting room for about five minutes when the nurse came in and told us that Naesha's heart had stopped, but she assured us that they got it to start beating again. She too told us to keep praying. I had no idea that my sister had died. I could never tell her how she was the ultimate role model for me. How sometimes I envied her resilience, the way she could be knocked down by situations in life and come back stronger every single time. I almost lost a pillar in my life that day. A pillar who didn't even know how important she was to me because I never told her.

While Naesha was in recovery, none of the doctors thought she would make it. Dr. Kamath stayed with her that whole first night, and she wasn't doing well. I remember seeing the waiting room filled almost to capacity with people who loved Naesha; mostly there just praying and being supportive for her family. It always amazes me how many people she knows. Since my mom and I knew she wouldn't want people to see her like she was in the hospital, we darn near stood guard at the recovery room to make sure no one came to see her without our permission. It was difficult, but we managed. I made sure that nobody cried while they were in the room with her, because I didn't want her to be worried or scared while she was sedated. She always said how well I could sing, so I sang a song for my sister every day when she was in a medically induced coma.
I remember when Naesha woke up from her coma.

It was that very day that I made a practice to tell her that I love her, and to hug and kiss her before I left her room. My mom and I basically moved in with her from that point on. When she was in the hospital, we had a room that they actually rented out to families whose relatives were staying for long periods of time. When she went home, I manned the upstairs while my mom took downstairs. I am thankful for my sister every day, and hope we can spend the rest of our lives telling each other that.

– Naeconda, sister

***

Day by day she improved, and slowly the machines and medications were removed. Nancy and I remained diligent guards at her door—even refusing entrance to some people. We were always in and out of her room. She was in a coma, but we would talk and talk to her. Her sister would sing to her. I'm not sure of the title, but it was a gospel song. One of the lines was, "I don't believe He brought me this far to leave me." To this day, I cry when I hear it. I made a recording of Sydney telling her mom she loved her and to hurry and get well, and also one of Reese crying. I wanted Naesha to hear and remember that she had two precious babies to live for. There was also a paper plate hanging over her bed that read: "Eat these words: I love you. Sydney"

It was a year or so later, sitting with a healthy Naesha, that I played her the recordings. She asked me to stop, but she remembered hearing them! Dr. Kamath helped bring our Naesha back to us. We thanked him over and over again then, as we still do now, but he said it was the man upstairs that saved her, and to thank Him. We do. Everyday.

— Apryl, godmother

***

June 2008. The Columbia County School System had completed another successful academic year. During the summer, we received word that one of our young up-and-coming administrators, Naesha Parks, had given birth to a very healthy baby boy. It was approximately two weeks later we received word that Naesha had been admitted to the hospital. We immediately assumed there must have been a setback with possible complications as result of the recent birth of her son. We later learned that Naesha had experienced what we were being told was a heart attack and that she would possibly need a heart transplant.

It was extremely difficult for me to imagine Naesha exhibiting any health-related problems. To see Naesha and to have conversation with her, you would quickly come to the conclusion that she was a very healthy young lady.

As the Superintendent of a large school system with approximately 24,000 students and over 3,000 employees, it was difficult to keep me abreast of the personal issues of this many people. However, as I mentioned earlier, Naesha had become an administrator of one of our elementary schools and was on track for a bright professional career.

I had asked my secretary to get daily updates on Naesha regarding her illness. With each passing day, it seemed the news regarding her illness and prognosis for recovery was getting worse. We were told that Naesha had undergone open-heart surgery and that additional complications were detected during the surgery. With the passing of days and having received word that Naesha was in a coma, we were told that we shouldn't expect her to live.

Upon hearing this news, I felt compelled to go to the hospital to visit Naesha, or at least visit with her family. I thought it was necessary for me to let the family know that her colleagues, her school family, and her students were praying for a full recovery.

When I arrived at the hospital, I was told that Naesha was not seeing any visitors and they could not give me any update on her condition. I asked the lady at the information desk if she would call the waiting room on Naesha's floor to see if any family member was present for me to talk with to at least to let them know someone from the school system had come by for a visit. After numerous attempts to call the waiting room on her floor had failed to get an answer, I decided to go the nurse's station on that floor to talk to a nurse or family member.

When I arrived at the nurse's station and inquired about Naesha, and also my desire to visit with her or a family member, I was immediately denied that request and politely asked to leave the floor. Being very understanding of the situation, I could appreciate the position of the hospital and respected the privacy they were providing their patient.

Even to this day, I cannot understand my persistence to see for myself how Naesha was doing on that day. I also can't explain why on an impulse I left my office to go to the hospital in the first place and why that day. As I previously stated, we have well over 3,000 employees of which many have been in the hospital for one reason or another and I have not visited with many of them except the few that were close friends of mine. I knew Naesha, but only for the short time she had been an administrator in the school system. Looking back now, I knew God had a purpose, but what?

Not being one to take no for an answer, I stated again to the head nurse to at least allow me to speak to a member of Naesha's family. And, again, I was told very politely they could not disturb the family and that I would need to leave.

As I left the nurse's station for the elevators, I was approached by another nurse that recognized me and knew that Naesha was an employee in our school system. She told me that it would not be ethical for her to discuss Naesha's condition but went on to say that they did not think her chance of survival was very good. Actually, there was only about a five percent or less chance she could make it. The nurse said she did not know a good reason for not allowing me to see Naesha for a brief moment. She told me that Naesha had been asleep for a good while and that it was unlikely she would wake up during my visit. I wanted to know if she was sleeping because of sedation or if she was she still in a coma. I never got to ask the question because I was being led quickly down the hallway to Naesha's room.

When the nurse first approached me and offered to take me to Naesha's room, I hesitated briefly. It was not because I didn't want to break hospital rules, but because I didn't know why I was being so persistent when all the news I had received was not very good. Also, I wasn't sure if I should intrude on her family when they were certainly struggling with Naesha's condition and prognosis.

As we approached the room, the nurse let me in and quickly closed the door and left. I knew then I was on my own. Naesha's sister, Naeconda, was asleep on a cot next to Naesha's bed. I learned later the other family members had gone home to get some rest and take care of the new baby and daughter.

I stood in that room for what seemed to be a long time. I could not get my head around the fact that this healthy person had given birth to a new son and had a daughter at home that needed her mother at her young impressionable age. However, I am a man of faith and I believe that there is a destined path that will make us stronger as we move forward with our lives. I also believe in prayer and it was at that time I took Naesha's hand and I began to pray and pray. I felt very strongly that God had a plan for this young lady. I felt strongly that the person whose hand I was holding was not the hand of someone who was dying. I think that I prayed as much for Naesha's two children as I did for Naesha. I especially prayed for her daughter Sydney. Sydney was about eight or nine years of age at the time and had already known her mother's love. I knew then that Naesha needed to get well for no other reason than to be there for Sydney.

As I stood at the bedside, Naeconda awakened and I quickly introduced myself because I knew I wasn't supposed to be in the room. I could tell I had startled her from what had been a brief night of sleep. Naeconda gave me an update of Naesha's condition and told me that Naesha had been asleep for a long time but the family had not given up hope.

As we were talking, I continued to hold Naesha's hand. It was at that time, and out of nowhere, that Naesha said, "Mr. Nagle, is that you?"

I immediately looked at Naesha as she opened her eyes and began focusing on me and the sound of my voice. After everything I had been told and what I had seen for myself, I couldn't believe the clarity in which we (she) spoke for the next several minutes. Before I left her hospital room, Naesha and I agreed and made a declaration it didn't matter how long it would take for her to get well and recuperate—she would get well and return to her family and to her career.

Not long after Naesha's health scare, she interviewed with me for a principal's position. Little did she know that her real interview took place at her hospital bedside many months earlier. As I stated previously, I am a man of faith, so who am I to stand in the way of destiny?

As superintendent, I meet regularly with our principals and school administrators. I have always given the opening remarks for the conference. My goal was to inspire the system and school administrators and encourage them to meet the challenges of their jobs with faith and conviction. I would try to instill in them that they all had significant roles to play to ensure total success of the system as well as meet their individual career goals.

Not long after Naesha returned work, I opened the school system's conference with my opening remarks to the 200 plus administrators. Inspiring that year was easier than most because my topic was The Naesha Parks story, AND, she was sitting with us that day! I appreciate Naesha for being an inspiration to me and I am proud that I forced my presence into her hospital room to witness God's miracle!

— Charles Nagle, superintendent

***

I began babysitting Sydney when she was in the third grade. Naesha had Saturday school on the weekends, so Sydney would stay with me. From there, our relationship grew. I kept Sydney practically the entire summer one year. She would occasionally come to my church on Sundays, and they both would stop to visit during our family functions at the house. During this time, Naesha and I grew closer as well. She became a positive female role model that I could have real one-on-one conversations with, other than my mother, and older sister. It also helped that she was in the field where I aspired to work. Naesha gave me important feedback about my academic career, and opportunities I should look for in the coming years.

I remember my mom coming home from work telling me Naesha was pregnant. I was sort of surprised; I didn't know she was trying. I continued to watch Sydney throughout the pregnancy. During this time, Naesha moved into a new house. We had candid conversations about life; Naesha told my mom and me about being prophesied to by Pastor McCoy. He told her that her mother would see God through her. She didn't know what that meant, or how it was even going to happen.

A few days before Naesha's scheduled C-section, she asked that I go to the store to stock up her fridge. She wanted there to be enough food in the house when the new baby arrived. My friend and I had the buggy full to capacity! When we arrived back to the house, and after putting the groceries away, Naesha told me I could join the family at the hospital to welcome baby Reese in the world. She told me to be at University Hospital early the morning of June 12th, and early I was. I was the only one in the waiting room! I dozed off as I waited. When I woke up, Keenan was just passing by saying Reese had been born. I got up and followed him in the room.

When both mommy and baby were reunited, Naesha unwrapped his blanket and counted his fingers and toes. Shortly after holding Reese for the first time, I left. I wanted them to have their bonding time.

Mommy and baby were sent home a few days

later. I want to say that the next Saturday, I received a call from my mom saying Naesha had to be rushed to the hospital. Because all of the adults were gone, I was the one who stayed with the children: Reese, Sydney, and Naesha's god-sister and brother, Courtney and Skylar. The next day I was downtown for my debutante meeting. A few minutes away from the hospital, I decided to stop by for a visit.

There were other people in the room. One I know was Yvette, as well as a fellow colleague from her doctorate class. She told us that while waiting at McDonald's with Yvette, Naesha had started to sweat. She got up and went to the restroom and had an out-of-body experience. She said it felt like an elephant was sitting on her chest. She knew something wasn't right. She went back out and told Yvette to dial 911 and told them to hurry. She recalled waking up that night with a slight pain in her leg. She got up and took an aspirin, something she doesn't usually do. Naesha was aware that her decision to take the aspirin is what probably saved her life.

A few moments later, the nurses let her mom sneak in the kids and baby Reese. I left and told them if they needed anything to just call me.

Well, I called the next day after church. I actually called a few times, but there was no response. Monday comes, and I still hadn't heard anything from her.

Around lunchtime, my mom called me with some news. She told me Yvette called and said Naesha was still in the hospital having some tests done. I knew Naesha was ready to go Saturday, she said she thought she'd be home by Sunday.

Time goes on, and then my dad came in. I remember it like it was yesterday. I was sitting on the floor in my mom's office, looking at some lipstick. Daddy says, "Naesha's still in the hospital."

I said, "Yea, I know."

Then he said, "She's not doing too good. Not doing good at all ... she might not make it."

Lost for words, all I could say was "Okay." But, there was a sense of peace in my mind. Every time I tried to process a funeral in my head, or even having to tell Sydney her mom was gone, it just didn't feel right. Without knowing the severity of the situation, I knew everything was going to be okay. That evening, Keenan asked if I could watch the kids. At this point, I became the official, unofficial babysitter for the next few weeks. Whenever I was needed, I was there.

I learned later what really took place that day: Sunday while getting some tests, doctors realized she needed a stent. From there everything went downhill. The doctors went up and told the family that there was a slim chance of survival. Within minutes, Naesha had coded. She needed a heart. She was out for sixteen whole minutes when the doctor questioned continuing working on getting her back. As we all know, he does, and at the twenty-third minute, the spirit of life resumed her body.

She was put in intensive care, where she stayed for a few weeks. Only close family and clergy could go down to see her. I snuck in one day when she finally made it to a room. Visitation was still limited, so I said I was her sister. Used to seeing a diva—a comical, vibrant, well-kept lady—reality hit when I saw the opposite. She wasn't vibrant; she was in and out of sleep. Her hair was out of tack, dark circles surrounded her eyes, and her nails had grown out. I told her all I wanted to do was say hey. I probably stayed all of two minutes.

Meanwhile, I was still watching the kids at the house. My parents and I would drop in occasionally when I was off duty, just to check on things. One Sunday after church we stopped by. Her mother and some others were there. As we were conversing about all that had taken place, her mother said, "I have seen God through Naesha." At that moment, my mind went back to that day Naesha, my mom, and I were having a conversation about the prophet telling her "Your mother will see God through you." Her mom said it word for word; she didn't even know she had just fulfilled a prophesy.

Naesha was able to come home before hers and Sydney's birthdays. There was a little gathering at her house. Again, we didn't stay long. This was a time for her and her family, especially the baby, to reconnect. In the days leading up to this transition, it was mentioned to my mom that it may be a good idea for me to stay with Naesha when everything came back to normal. It would be good to have someone else in the house to help, since Keenan worked out of town. I was about to be a senior in high school and loved my independence. I figured this would help my parents get used to an empty nest as I prepared myself for college. I didn't officially move in until October. I would still go home during the week to see my parents and gather some clothes. Other than that, Monday through Friday I lived with Naesha Parks.

One day we talked about what happened. She could recall a nurse coming in the room while she was recovering and saying, "You may not remember me, but I was the nurse that was by you as you said, 'Don't let me die. I have two kids at home. *Don't let me die.*' After the sixteenth minute, the doctor stopped and asked if he should stop working. I told him questions are not of God. So the doctor continued to work." After telling the story, she said she never saw that nurse again. When she asked the other nurses about her, they had no clue who she was talking about. An angel, perhaps?

On another occasion, she articulated about waking up out of her sleep and thinking the nurses let some kids climb and hang on the cabinets. When she focused her eyes, she saw this beautiful, bronzy angel with wings two times the angel's size. All the angel would say was, "Everything is going to be alright." Naesha went back and forth with angel, pleading she wasn't ready to die, she had children at home, she was not ready to die. All the angel would say was, "Everything is going to be alright." This exchange was said to have gone on for about thirty minutes, after which Naesha fought to go to sleep. When she woke up, they moved her into a regular room.

As my senior year went on, Naesha grew stronger. She got better. She began working again. Before you knew it, a year had gone by. Naesha supported me with all of my major senior year events. She was one of the first to find out about my scholarship and decision to attend the Fort Valley State University; she was there to send me off for prom, and for graduation. I stayed with her up until the week before I had to leave for college. To this day, we maintain a close relationship.

– Christina Perry, family friend

***

I remember getting off the plane having just returned from a conference and was told by Ann that Naesha was extremely sick. We went to the hospital and her family was there. I remember her mom being extremely upset. She had her close friend along with other family and friends there. I greeted everyone and then was allowed to go back to see Naesha. She was surrounded by nurses and laid out with her chest cavity open. I remember thinking, *Lord, this young mom.* I then took her hand and prayed for a miracle.

Most of my visits were basically the same, a lot of people in the waiting room and I would go back and pray. It was amazing to see she was gradually getting better.

Oh, there was one more memory. I remember going to visit and she was alert. She had a very seemingly scared look on her face as she told me what she experienced in her near death experience. I remember that Naesha was acutely aware of the fact that that she had experienced a miracle. That was a very powerful moment that I shall never forget!

I remember a discussion with Naesha about dying. After her close event with death, she was understandably very fearful. I told her that what she needed to focus on was living and that dying would take care of itself. I really think at first she was uneasy with what I was saying so I explained further. I said to her that she had already done something that many people will never experience. My feeling was, if God wanted her at that point He would have taken her, but for some reason He allowed her to stay. He answered many prayers that were sent up on her behalf. I explained that there had to be a reason that

God touched and chose her for this miracle and that now she needs to make the best of the rest of her life. I shared with her that she now had the tremendous task of sharing her experience with the world.

I wanted to give Naesha a sense of "miracle responsibility"; I feel that when God grants a miracle, He expects the recipient to take advantage of it. To spread the word of the goodness and the grace of God. Yes, there is a cost. There is a responsibility to being blessed. God does nothing just to be doing it. He always has a divine plan and purpose and He has chosen to use her. That is what I wanted her to carry from that conversation.

You will never know what God will do in an event in life. One thing that developed out of this situation is a closeness between Naesha and my daughter, Christina. She saw Naesha as a big sister, and I saw my daughter grow through this very painful situation. Christina stayed with Naesha almost a year in order to help her with the kids. Christina saw Naesha go through this experience and I think she grew. It forced her to be even more responsible and to gain even more focus in her life. I think at first Christina was scared, but after a few weeks she became comfortable and was honored to be able to help.

I was rather proud to see her rise to the occasion. She was already pretty mature, but this situation thrust her to a new level. She really respected Naesha and wanted to help in any way that she could and so this was indeed a win-win situation. I am sure that this will be a time in Christina's life that she will never forget. You never really know where or when you will learn life lessons, but when you get them, they stick. This will stick with her forever and I think it will make her a better person.

— Roscoe Perry, family friend

***

I had been friends with Dr. Naesha Parks for six years when she was hospitalized after giving birth to her son, Reese.

My oldest daughter, Wendy, called me and stated that Naesha had to be rushed to the hospital. Naesha had been home after giving birth to Reese for about nine days. I went to the hospital to visit Naesha and she was telling me the story about how she had been cooped up at the house and a friend came by and took her for a ride in order to get something to drink and to get out of the house. Naesha told me that "she had this weird feeling that she never experienced before." Naesha had sent for her laptop and someone was bringing it in. She kept making the statement that, she didn't want to die, and she wanted to be able to raise her two children. I kept wondering why she was making these statements over and over. I smiled and said, "Naesha you will be fine."

Naesha had a lot of visitors in her hospital room so I told her that I was getting ready to go and I would see her tomorrow. Naesha asked me if I would drop her daughter, Sydney, off at her godmother's house. I said, "Yes." As I hugged her and said that I would see her tomorrow, she made that statement again, "I do not want to die." I left Naesha in good hands with her Mom and family members but as I dropped her daughter off at her godmother's house, the statement Naesha made kept racing through my mind. I wanted to turn around and go back to the hospital and stay the night with her. I know how protective her family is about her, so I decided to go home.

The next day, I got a phone call, again from my oldest daughter stating that Naesha was in danger and they were getting ready to do surgery on her. My daughter stated, "Mom this is serious." My daughter knows how I will go in denial and not face the truth. I lost a good friend this way. My mind was totally confused. A friend of my daughter that worked at the hospital had given my daughter this message in order to get it to me. I rushed to the hospital and Naesha had just gone in for surgery. I could not get any answers from her family because they were all upset. Finally, Naesha's husband's grandmother told or explained to me what had happened. The waiting room was packed. I did what's best when there's a crisis. I prayed to myself, but I felt like we needed more. I asked for the hospital chaplain, but he had not arrived in the room yet. I got on my cell phone and called our pastor, Pastor Mitchell. Pastor Mitchell answered his phone and I told him we needed him and that Naesha was in surgery. I explained the circumstances to him. We did not have a good connection on the phone, but Pastor Mitchell told me that he was out of town but he would get one of the elders of the church over. Sure enough, two of the elders and their wives came to the hospital. The elders came so fast that it was hard to believe that they arrived as quickly as they did. The elders did pray with the family/friends that were in the family room. I mean they sent up a prayer where you couldn't help but feel God's presence in the room. The family seemed more at peace then. The elders of Restoration Ministries sent up a strong powerful prayer and we had prayer after prayer from other representatives. We needed this prayerful gathering because my friend was in trouble.

The nurses said that while they were getting her ready for surgery, Naesha made that same statement, "I do not want to die." My daughter's friend who was a nurse kept us informed about the surgery. The nurse friend told me that this was serious and Naesha was in good hands with Dr. Kamath. I knew my friend was in trouble and the seriousness of this surgery. The nurse friend told me a little about what was going on during the surgery. I called some of my friends that are prayer warriors all over the United States. I thought to myself, *Lord, please do not let me lose another friend.* Naesha was a good friend and a loyal one. Naesha would give you the coat off her back. She did not deserve this. The thought of losing her and for her not to be here to raise her two children was too much to bear.

The surgeon, Dr. Kamath, came in and talked to the family. He hugged Naesha's mom and her husband's grandmother. He talked to us calmly and seriously. He seemed very emotional while talking to the family. He said that Naesha was in trouble. It had taken him twenty-five minutes to revive her. He stated that tonight would be a critical time for her. Dr. Kamath also said that he'd lost her even before surgery, but he remembered her words: "Please do not let me die."

He kept trying to revive her and her heart started to beat and he placed her on the heart-lung bypass machine. He left her chest cavity open in case he needed to go back in. He also told the family that he was going to call around for a heart transplant because she was so young. He told the family that he was not leaving the hospital that night and he would be there to watch her. The family was very appreciative. My nurse friend told me that, "It did not look good and most people do not survive this type of surgery." My eldest daughter tried to prepare me for the worst. She said, "Mom even if she survives this, you know that she will have some type of brain damage because she stopped breathing for some time, I think twenty-five minutes." I know myself that usually after so many minutes after a person stops breathing they are pronounced dead. Dr. Kamath kept working with Naesha because God told him to. This was indeed a miracle about to happen and for all of us to witness.

There was a team of health care professionals taking care of Naesha around the clock. The surgeon stayed at her side also; he stayed all night.

Pastor Mitchell finally arrived and just missed the surgeon talking with the family. He came over to me and I pointed out Naesha's mom, husband, and sister. He went over to speak with the family after talking with the elders and me. I tried to give Pastor Mitchell as much information as I could concerning how Naesha ended up in the hospital nine days after giving birth to her newborn. Pastor Mitchell prayed with the family and Naesha's mom said that she even felt better after his prayer.

My friend was still in the ICU and only immediate family and pastors could go in and visit with her for a short period. They did not want anyone to visit long with Naesha. She was still in a medically induced coma.

I went to visit the family at the hospital every morning and after work. I asked if there was anything I could do to help them. I called the church and Pastor Mitchell also informed the church to send food over for the family at the hospital. Naesha's family asked if I could go over and keep the baby in the afternoon so that her husband could come and visit Naesha at the hospital. Of course, I said, yes. Every afternoon I would go to Naesha's house to keep her children. My daughters were so helpful; they assisted me in helping with the newborn. Friends, teachers, and church family groups were so nice in making sure food, drinks, diapers, and other things were available for Naesha's children at the house.

I finally went in to see Naesha and wished that I had not. I could not get close to her to give her a hug or kiss. I stood at the foot of her bed and watched her. Someone said a prayer and the next thing I knew, her sister was singing. I tuned in to help sing. I am not a singer, but I was led by God. When I left Naesha's room, I broke down and cried. That was the first time that I had seen her during this ordeal. Reality really set in and I was afraid. After my tears, I had to get myself together; to be strong for her and her family. I look strong and may even seem strong during crisis, but I was hurting too. Again, I called for prayers. My confidence was down again. I did not want to lose her. *If she would just open her eyes.*

Pastor Mitchell visited with Naesha and with her family. He said that she would live and be a witness to others by her life situation. I felt better in hearing him say this. Naesha did wake up and we were all joyful. They did a series of tests on her and she passed them all with flying colors. She was moved to a private room. Again, only immediate family were allowed to see her. I gave the family that respect. I called Naesha and talked with her a few minutes. She said that she was wondering where I was. I told her that I would come by to see her. I went by to visit her, but did not stay long at all. They were getting her out of bed to walk and I did not want to disturb her.

I did not see Naesha again until she went home. I went to visit her to give her and her daughter's birthday present. Naesha wanted to talk about her surgery ordeal, but her mom said that it was too soon, so we talked about other things. Naesha was a little depressed, because she could not remember anything and was wondering why she was in the shape that she was in. She was even asking, "Why me?"

When her family members told her a little about the surgery, Naesha was very grateful for her family, friends, church members, pastors, husband, and children during the time she was in surgery.

As Naesha was healing, at times she would make the statement, "I wonder if I should have gotten pregnant." She was putting the blame on being pregnant or the baby. Naesha's mom stated firmly, "Will this child ever be able to live this down? You need to stop saying this."

This definitely got Naesha's attention and made her think. Naesha stopped making these statements. We all witnessed a miracle before our eyes, and my friend is still with me and I cherish her friendship every day. Naesha has made great achievements since her surgery in so many ways. God is still working in her life and she is a witness for Him. Naesha was working on her doctoral degree and has gone on to earn and receive her doctorate in Education/Leadership. We are very proud of the leadership skills she has and for letting God shine through her.

> *"A friend loveth at all times"*
>
> Proverbs 17:17

– Joyce Cox, family friend

***

I recall being at home with my two children enjoying our summer break when I got the call from a co-worker about Naesha being in the hospital and that it was something that involved her heart and that the prognosis was not looking good. I remember having a feeling of shock, being scared for her, and having a lot of questions. I remember praying for Naesha immediately and asking God to heal her from whatever was going on.

As the days passed, I found out the details of what had happened to Naesha in the days that followed after having Reese. I could not believe what I was hearing and how bleak it was looking. I felt helpless! I was thinking to myself, *What can I do to help besides pray?* Another co-worker and I decided to take dinner to Keenan and see if he needed any help with Reese and Sydney. When we walked into the house and saw that sweet baby boy in his daddy's arms, I had to hold back tears. All I could think was, *Here is a newborn baby who needs his mama and she is in the hospital fighting for every breath she takes.* I was heartbroken. I remember holding Reese in my arms and rocking him for a little while before leaving and noticing that Sydney was very quiet and mostly staying in her room.

After visiting for a while and seeing what we could do to help, we told Keenan to let us know if we could do anything for him and that we would continue to pray. As I was getting in the car, I had to fight back tears as I cried out loud to God saying, "Please DO NOT take this mama from these precious children!" Each day that passed, I would get updates and would hope and pray for a good report. There were good days and bad days for Naesha, and as the weeks went on, she fought and became stronger and stronger. I never stopped praying because I am a strong believer in the power of prayer. I knew each time that I got an update that she was getting stronger and better; she was truly a miracle from God, and I gave Him all of the praise.

When she finally was able to return to school, she told us her story and the journey that she had been through. I don't think there was a dry eye in the room when she told us the story from the beginning to the end, and there were many times when I had chill bumps on my arms from the stories that she told about seeing the angel and the vivid details of her face, wings, and size. I can still visualize it today! I am thankful that Naesha is here to tell her story.

– Angie Young, colleague

III

"We can do all things through Christ who strengthens us."

Philippians 4:13

I WAS FINALLY ON my way to recovery. One might ask where my spiritual strength came from. It certainly wasn't by any power of my own. I suppose it began at the age of twelve, when I gave my life to Christ and was baptized outside under a small blue and white tent in the small town of Thomson. Apostle Daryl McCoy (my spiritual father) preached a message so powerful that I literally saw God that night. I knew that I needed to hear from Him. So right after my move to the regular floor at the hospital, I felt strongly that I needed to speak with Apostle McCoy. He would have a word from God.

My family tried to contact him. In the meantime, I

wouldn't allow myself to fall asleep. The paralyzing fear in the room would not allow me to sleep. I remembered my encounter with the angel. As beautiful as she was, I didn't want to die just yet.

After many attempts, Apostle McCoy was on the phone. My sister spoke to him briefly to let him know of my medical condition and then she handed me the phone. I spoke these words to him: "They are telling me that I died and that I have had open heart surgery. I'm scared, I don't want to die. I want to live."

He told me to hear the word of the Lord, "You Shall Live and NOT die." He prayed a prayer just as powerful as the message he preached the night that I gave my life to Christ. I saw God again. Before ending the conversation with him, he told me to rest in the peace of God. He asked me if I believed in him as a man of God. I answered with a simple yes. He said that he loved me and told me to go to sleep.

Inwardly, I began to praise God. I thanked him for giving me the miracle I didn't deserve. I told Him, "You have done so much for me. Tell me Lord, what I can do for you?"

The spirit of the Lord came to me and told me to "raise my son like Joshua."

I kept waiting, waiting for the angel to appear again even in my dreams. I remembered everything about her eyes, her color, and her size. I felt certain that she would come for me again. She never did. Inside, I think I may have known that she wasn't going to visually manifest herself, but her spirit never really left.

The last time that I remembered seeing my husband was the day that I left to go McDonald's with my friend. My son, then only ten days old, was lying on his Bumbo, and my husband was on his computer. Walking out of the door that day was the same as every other. Little did I know that it would be months before I returned home and that I would never return to life as I knew it.

After the coma, I remember my husband walking into my hospital room. The moment we made eye contact, he began to cry. My husband rarely cries, if ever at all. I asked, "Why, are you crying?"

His voice strained, he said, "I never thought that I would ever see you like this again." When reflecting on his strength and courage, I use the following analogy: while I was fighting for my life, my husband was fighting to keep our newborn son perfect. Keeping him perfect is exactly what he did. I once heard that compared to a woman, it is impossible for a man to be everything that a newborn baby needs. Without a doubt, I can say that the love of a father will bring out every gift in a man that is necessary to preserve the integrity of his family and protect his children. I was so proud of what he'd done, but he was ready for me to come home.

Hour after hour, it became apparent that the focus

of everyone in my room was preparing me for that one task that seemed so far away—going home. In my mind, I wondered who would be with me and how I would survive without twenty-four hour care. The thought of not having a button to push to call for a nurse literally left me physically sick and helpless. Why was God clipping my wings?

Early one morning while my mother was reading scriptures, a woman came into the room dressed in scrubs. Her face was covered in moles and she had a white net on her head. She said, "I couldn't leave today without stopping by to let you know that you are a living miracle. In all the years I've worked with Dr. Kamath, he had never asked me if he should stop resuscitating."

She continued, "I want you to know that on minute sixteen, he looked at me and asked if I thought he should stop. I told him, 'Usually when you have a question about something, its doubt and not of God. Remember what she told you—she asked you not to let her die. Keep going.'" He did and after about twenty minutes or so, my heart began to beat again. She left me with these words: "To whom much is given, much is required."

I spent my days and nights trying to remember the events that led me to the place that I was in. There was a range of emotions: rage, fear, gratitude, disappointment, and most of all, anger. One day, while feeling an abundant amount of anxiety, a strikingly tall, dark man with a white coat walked into my room. I later learned that after being told that we could not switch to one of the most well-known cardiologists, my mother tracked this man down as he was making his rounds: Dr. Andrew MacBowman. Although hospital staff told her that she could not switch cardiologists, she stopped him and introduced herself. Her words to the doctor were, "My daughter needs YOU." He agreed and told her the protocol needed to change cardiologists.

Our first verbal exchange was a little unorthodox. Before he said anything medically related, he spoke these words over my life and into my then failing heart. He said, "Ms. Parks, I don't know what God has for you, but I am honored to be a part of it." He would become much more than a doctor; he would become a friend. There are truly no accidents in God. Dr. Bowman was from the same town as my parents, played football with my dad, and we later learned his sister was a high school friend of my mothers. In so many words, God was establishing the foundation for my miracle well before any medical intervention would be needed. Because of this friendship, he helped to build my confidence in being able to go home.

I recall the day I walked through the front door of my home after leaving the hospital. Either everything about home was different or I had really changed. Outside I was smiling, but inside I was in a whirlwind of doubt. This just wasn't fair. Unanswered questions flooded my mind: *Who would I call on for help? Who would teach me how to take care of myself? Who would give me my medicine?* At that moment, if I could have, I would have turned around and gone back to my "safe" place: the hospital. I couldn't go back, though; that wasn't an option.

I went home with a 2-3 inch hole in my chest that hadn't closed. It would have to be flushed and packed daily. I had in-home therapy and a nurse that would come by twice a week. While I was very thankful for being alive, inside I questioned whether the life ahead of me would be worth living. My mother and sister split up the hours so that I would have someone with me every day and night. I had no idea that I would spend the next couple of months taking one step forward and two steps back.

I had forgotten what it was like to sleep in my own bed. My mother and husband would put me in bed at night, wake me up in the morning, and literally force me to begin my day. I wanted to sleep through the nightmare of this life and wake up with everything the same as it was. I didn't have an appetite, so I would force myself to eat. After eating, the time I hated most would come—time for me to take medicine. I totally resented having to take twenty pills. Prior to my surgery, I never had to take any medicine at all. I flat out refused to learn my medicine routine, as if my noncompliance would punish the person responsible for this tragedy. The only problem was that I had no one to blame. My inward defiance to learn was fear-based. I was afraid that if I was able to do it myself that my mother and sister would leave and I would be left to resume my nightmarish life with no nurses. The thought was terrifying. I knew how to live as the old Naesha. I didn't want to learn to be this new, but not improved, version. I kept looking for excuses instead of looking for a way to pick up the pieces and move forward.

After taking the pills, I had a full day of therapy. A number of therapists came to the house. One came to assist me with walking and exercises for my legs to help with blood flow and increase my balance. Day by day, I began to get a little more independent.

Once I became more mobile, I could get up on my own and take care of my own hygiene. The one thing that I wasn't able to do yet was take care of my son. At night, I would get in the bed on my own. My mother would sleep in the bed with me. She would put my son in between us. It was horrible not to be able to snuggle and cuddle him, but I was comforted just knowing that he was there.

As I transitioned into my new life, I would look at my beautiful son and I am ashamed to say that I harbored resentment toward him at times. Many nights, as he lay next to me in bed, I would cry out to God about my son. I felt that if I had never gotten pregnant, never given birth, I wouldn't be living inside this prison. Instead of thanking God that he was a healthy little man, I was asking God to take the resentment away so that I could properly bond with my baby. It wasn't his fault that this had happened to me, but I was having a hard time accepting that reality.

Days, weeks, and months went by and I became stronger. My mother went home. Reese and I bonded. My husband resumed his normal routine. He worked away from home and would come home on Friday night and leave Sunday night. I was still very insecure and never wanted to be alone. I played the movie that featured something happening to me, and my kids having to watch me take my last breath, over and over in my mind. That wasn't how I wanted them to remember their mommy.

God knows just what we need and when we need it. I was introduced to a young lady who would become another member of my family. She would be there to pick me up when I was falling. When I needed someone to help and support us, she was right there. She moved into my house and spent her entire senior year with me. I felt a surreal peace when she was there. God knew just what I needed and He sent me Christina. She shared with me that she looked at me as a role model. What she saw on the outside was a strong, confident person. Inwardly, I was afraid to embrace my new normal.

As the weeks and days went by, and after countless hours of therapy, it was time for me to go back to work. Throughout my recovery process, I thought about all the students and teachers who wrote and encouraged me on a regular basis. There were times that I felt like I never wanted to go back to work and then there were times that I felt that my life wouldn't be complete unless I went back.

Panic attacks were an additional hurdle in my recovery. I knew I had to get them under control before I returned to work. They were at their worst whenever I got behind the wheel of a car. In fact, my first panic attack occurred when I was driving to my mother's house to visit. I was talking to God questioning why I had to go through something so traumatic. Tears were rolling down my face like the water from Niagara Falls. I just could not stop the tears from flowing. My son was in his car seat chewing on a toy, and my daughter was sitting beside him with her headphones on. They were doing exactly what children their ages do. They were fully engaged in their own world. Neither of them were aware that their mother was sobbing uncontrollably in the front seat. I arrived at my mother's, and my daughter finally noticed my tears. She asked what was wrong, but before I could respond, she opened the truck door and ran inside to get my mother. Sydney was in complete shock. She had a vision of me as being as strong as a rock. I was the one who managed to make everything in her life okay. It seemed as though she did what she knew how to do. Run.

Once my mother came outside to my truck that was still running, she could barely understand what I was saying. I was still weeping profusely. I looked up at the sky, and in a loud cry, I yelled, "I just want to take care of my kids and meet my grandchildren."

She held me and hugged me as tightly as she had when I was a child. She rocked and comforted me, saying, "You will. I promise, you will."

If I could recapture the feeling of security that I felt in that moment, I would be able to endure and come back to myself again. I managed to calm down and get out of the truck. I eventually had to take medicine to control my anxiety. I was extremely worried about fully recovering. I wanted to reclaim my life. I just didn't know how to.

One Sunday, not long after, my mother and I were visiting my grandmother's church. As the service came to an end, the pastor asked me to come forward. He said these words. "You will live and not die. God told me to tell you that you WILL meet your grandchildren." What a word. How did this young pastor, whom my mother and I had never met, know my most intimate thoughts? Prior to that day at my mother's, I had never expressed my fears about meeting my grandchildren. I tended to focus on the obstacles that were directly in my current path like raising my own children. That concern was between me and God, or at least I thought so. God heard every word that day at my mother's, and He was trying to send a word that confirmed that He would get the glory from my story.

I continued trying to move forward. I had to make this all right for my children. They needed a mother. I did all the things my cardiologist recommended, one of which was to press through the panic attacks. He advised me to get back into the routine of things. When I felt myself having a panic attack or getting upset, especially in the car, I should turn the air vents directly on my face and breathe slowly. Day after day, I continued to do just that. My panic attacks got less and less frequent.

I followed his plan while driving to cardiac rehabilitation. My husband and I had enrolled our son in a Christian daycare located along the same route I would take to get to there. The goal was to get my son and me in the routine of a daily schedule before I started back to work. I was traveling down the road that the daycare was on. Interestingly enough, there was a funeral home located right next to the daycare. Seeing that took me back to my experience and how I almost died. I would vividly imagine my family lined up outside and my body in a casket with my children crying next to it. I felt a panic attack slowly approaching. There was a lot of stop-and-go traffic because the area was surrounded by shopping stores and food establishments. As I prayed to God, I began questioning His purpose for allowing me to experience such trauma. This was not supposed to happen. I began to cry out to God almost as if I was demanding that He speak back to me. I was passing by a Chik-fil-a, saying loudly, "Why me, God? I've tried to live my life serving you. I'm not the chief of sinners. I know people who have murdered others and don't have to go through anything like this." I was so furious with Him. *Why me?* In that moment, I could hardly catch my breath and my whole life seemed to flash before my eyes.

Then, in an audible voice, I heard these words. "Why not you? This was never about *you*." I immediately looked at my radio. Maybe the words came from there. Perhaps I had forgotten to turn the radio off. Surely, there was an explanation. Wasn't there?

The radio was off, per doctor's orders. I almost ran my truck off the road. Startled and afraid, I gazed to the second and third row of my truck. Did someone sneak into my car? Who is this person in my car? There was no one. Then came a strong sense of peace. Once again, the voice of God had spoken, so I certainly planned to listen. I got it! How many lives had my story impacted? How many relationships did my trauma heal? Yes, I was driving the vehicle, but God was the voice. My test was to develop my testimony. This was an experience meant to impact the world. This event, though traumatizing, was never about *me*. It was about the world understanding that God is the same today, yesterday, and forevermore.

The day arrived that I had to go back to work. I would work half-days for month or so until I could physically handle being at work all day long. When I was finally able to work a full day, it was interrupted by a two-hour break for me to leave and go to cardiac rehab. Cardiac rehab was hard for me. It reminded me of how young I was compared to the other people who were there. I would always get the comment, "You are too young to have had a heart attack." I would then have to tell them my story to help them move past my age and understand that I was not any different from them. Each day on my drive to the hospital, I would thank God that I was alive to drive and that maybe my story had inspired hope for the others in cardiac rehab, or at least was a story of caution to the young women in their lives.

I specifically remember meeting a gentlemen who would add to my story of miracles. Having been back at work for about a month, I found myself extremely behind and pushing myself to get caught up. Wow, was I drowning. I was working hard to gather information that my principal needed. Then, after compiling the information for him, I quickly left my office and went to his. I walked out the door and there was a man just standing in the doorway, looking as if he had seen a ghost. He was average height and had vibrant red hair. Tears rolled down his face. I asked, "Sir, is everything okay? Is there something that I can do for you?"

Pale, he asked, "You have no idea who I am, do you?"

Inwardly, I thought this was a parent who was upset because of a consequence that I gave his child, or maybe he was someone who was unhappy about something a teacher did. Once my thoughts settled, I realized that I did not know who the man was or what he could possibly want.

To prevent distraction, I beckoned him to step inside my office. He said, "I was your very first nurse after your surgery. My name is Lucky. I want you to know how hard we worked to keep you stable. My wife had just had a baby, and as I was taking care of you, all I could think about was her. There were many nights that I stayed at your beside and prayed to God that He would let you live. You are here and you are well." He told me that I probably would never remember him because they were giving me a white milky substance called propafol to keep me in the coma, and it affects your memory. He was so shaken. Finally, his daughter arrived at the front office and he left.

As soon as he was gone, the magnitude of my situation hit me again. I knew that my story needed to be told and that there were many facets that would evolve along my journey. I called my mom and couldn't get an answer. I called my sister and she picked up. By this time, I was crying. It's hard for me to describe exactly what I was feeling. I suppose it was a mixture of gratitude and uncertainty. How many people were out there that could add to my experience? How was it possible for me to not remember a thing about who this man was?

My sister asked, "What's wrong? What's wrong?"

I said, "Who was my first nurse when I was in the coma?"

She laughed. "His name was Lucky," she said. "Momma and I thought it was very ironic that the first nurse assigned to you was 'Lucky.' We took that as a sign," she said. It was more like fate instead of luck. It was God's way of sending His message of hope.

One day, my boss came in and sat in my office. He said, "I don't know why I want to do this, but I think I want to transfer to another school. You're ready," he said. Inside, there was a multitude of doubt. I wasn't ready for more responsibility. He couldn't leave now. I thought I needed a little more time. However, he thought that there wasn't a better time than now, and so he transferred.

I remember feeling a cloud of peace when I interviewed for the principal job. I felt that I was going to go into the interview with the panel of ten or fifteen parents and teachers in the room, and give them all the right answers. Each of them was very formally dressed, and outside the room was the Director of Human Resources. He walked over to tell me that it was my turn to interview. I entered the conference room, and all of the faces were familiar. They asked all the textbook questions, and I answered them all to the best of my knowledge.

Finally, they asked "the question." They asked why I was the right person for the job. I paused and prayed inwardly because my honest answer might be quite different from any of the other candidates. I answered by saying this: "I asked myself the very same question over and over again. I could give you a textbook answer, or I can answer the question from my heart. I chose the latter. Over the last year, I have been fighting for my life. There were times when I thought the world would be better off without me. However, one day I realized that my journey wasn't just about me. I pressed play to see the movie in my mind where all the school psychologists gathered at the school to tell my students that their principal didn't make it. I had to hit stop each time because that wasn't how I wanted this to end. What about the students whom I told that I would see when I got back from having my baby? What about the little girls who waited on me every morning to see what kind of shoes that I was wearing? What about the kids who needed to see my face in the mornings so that they could have a good day? I fought to get back to these kids and I will continue to fight to do what is in their best interest. Their love was what kept me strong throughout the process and they deserve to have a happy ending. I am the best person for the job because I am their principal."

By this time, there wasn't a dry eye in the room. Someone sent out for a box of Kleenex. I apologized for making them cry, thanked them for the opportunity, and walked away. When I walked out of the conference room,

I thanked God and asked Him to move on my behalf if the position was for me.

To be honest, I hadn't given the position much thought and I received a phone call from the Director of Human Resources asking me to meet him at the board meeting where he would be presenting the council's unanimous recommendation to appoint me the new principal of my school. I thanked him and gave praise to God. My students would finally get their happy ending.

IV

*"To know wisdom and instruction; to perceive
the words of understanding."*

Proverbs 1:2

Dear Naesha,

Last year at this time, Scott called from the beach to tell me what had happened to you. The only number he had was Mark's and somehow Mark had mine. I couldn't believe how sick you were. Scott wanted me to call everyone and let them know. I started calling the phone tree list. Most people didn't answer, but I left messages just to pray for you. When anyone asked what they could do I just told them to pray. The ones that got messages started calling me back. Again, I told them that all we could do was pray. Many folks told me they had not been able to sleep well and had prayed for you each time they awoke in the middle of the night. This was my experience also. For several nights whenever I would wake I would pray for your strength to return. Many, many people prayed for your healing throughout the day and night!

When I talked to Karrie Hendrick we decided we needed to do more—but what? We figured that you may have lots of folks at your house and maybe paper goods would be materials we could provide. Karrie and I went shopping and brought those things to your house. We met Keenan and Reese. Of course, we had to hold Reese and get that good baby love. We both were impressed with Keenan and how much love and concern that he showed. People kept calling and emailing. I told them all to pray. People dropped off stuff at my house for you. Angie and I came and brought these things to your house. And we kept praying.

And our prayers were answered! Slowly you began to regain your strength. We all witnessed your miracle healing and saw the power of prayer first hand!

And here we are a year later ...

– Marilyn Huff, colleague

* * *

Naesha and I have known each other for ten years. We didn't date long before marriage. It was a "whirlwind romance." I was working at the ASU literacy center. One day, Naesha called wanting to sign her daughter, Sydney ,up with the tutoring center. I don't know how it started, but the conversation was easy, and we talked for two hours on work time. If my boss had known, he probably would have fired me.

I realized our conversation was coming to an end, and the only thing I could think to do was offer her tickets I had to the circus. She said she'd stop by and pick them up the next day. We've been together ever since.

I was at home with Reese when Naesha got sick. Yvette picked her up to get her out of the house. She was getting stir crazy. I can't remember who called but it was either a friend or Naesha's mom who called and told me she was on her way to the hospital. At the time, I wasn't really alarmed. I just thought it was a post-partum complication. I thought she was just taking precautions and going to the hospital. I asked if I needed to get over there right then, and they said no, just stay with the baby.

It wasn't until she was being admitted that I began to worry.

I was really concerned and no one knew what her condition was. I didn't have time to process; everything moved so quickly for me. I was really more scared about being alone with the baby for an extended period of time. I was confused, but wasn't thinking about what was really going on. I was thinking in the moment. My wife was in the hospital, I had the baby, and I didn't know who needed me more. But I figured her godmother was with her, and there were others to take care of her, so I stayed at home with Reese. I didn't even go visit the hospital on Friday.

On Saturday, Naesha was still able to communicate, so I took Reese to the hospital. Naesha had this urgent look in her eyes. She looked worn out, but she had concern on her face and said to me, "Take care of my baby."

I didn't have a whole lot of support with Reese at first, because nobody had any idea the extent of the illness. It was scary to be at home by myself and I didn't have much newborn experience. I was extra careful about everything where Reese was concerned. Even diaper changes. I knew that if anything went wrong, Naesha would know immediately when she got home. I was off from work for two weeks to focus on taking care of the baby anyway. What I didn't expect was the loneliness. I worked out of town and was home on the weekends, so I was used to not being around her all the time. But this was a little different.

On Sunday, we went through the normal process with the baby. I think it was early afternoon that I got a call from my mother-in-law, saying that Naesha was going to have emergency open-heart surgery. I was stunned. She had been okay the day before and now she was on her deathbed. She had coded and they were trying to revive her. I was going about 120 mph to the hospital to figure out what was going on. She'd had a heart attack.

The doctor came in and confirmed this. He gave basic information, but expressed the need to get her immediately into surgery. I started bawling. I didn't know what was going on. I thought the C-section put her down a little bit, but that she'd be fine. Nothing compared to that feeling. Not even death. Everyone that's been close to me is still alive. And then to have to make a decision about how to keep her alive? Hardest thing I've ever experienced.

I think I dealt with it better than everyone else, but I was scared. I felt this pride of being in control, not wanting to be dependent on others. I had to make decisions for the family, but I wanted to *do* something. But there was nothing to be done except get on my knees and pray. I couldn't make her feel better at all. Typically, when I've been faced with adversity, I take ten seconds, then push it away and move on. But I couldn't. There was literally nothing to do except pray. In that moment, I wasn't worried about my kids. All I could think about was what I could do to help save my wife's life. I wiped the tears and prayed. One thing I know about her is that she's a fighter. She's a leader. I asked God to guide the doctor's hands, to do what needs to be done. I hadn't gotten to see her beforehand, and I prayed all the harder because of it.

Apparently, the cardiologist was going to put in a stent, and then he realized that it was much worse than they originally feared. Dr. Kamath was on "D" and he was one of the best cardiac surgeons in the world. My grandmother, a former LPN, had a personal relationship with Mac Bowman, and she was able to change cardiologists. It was a mess in the beginning, but all the stars aligned.

I stayed home with Reese during the surgery. I worked for Bluebird at the time, and they let me work from home. I was a buyer for manufacturing, so I didn't need to physically go into the office. My days were spent caring for Reese and working. Reese didn't like to sleep. I usually worked until 5:00 and then was with Reese. So many people came over and helped. When I was relieved around 4:30 or 5, I would go to hospital and stay until 10, then I'd go home and be up with Reese at night.

Naesha's godmother stayed with her during open-heart recovery. The pastor came in and prayed. Everyone got over the initial shock and then everyone was all about making sure everyone else was okay. Naesha is strong, and her godmother helped to keep everyone calm. Terrifying as it was, this event changed my relationship with her mom and some other family members. Nancy and I are ideal mother-in-law/son-in-law types; she loves everyone all over the place. She saw me and helped. I'd visit and tell Naesha to pull through this. There were no more tears allowed in the recovery room.

Her godmother, mom, and sister were like the hostesses of the recovery room. People you don't know come up to you, and you have to meet everyone. I wanted to go into a dark corner and cry, but I had to meet and greet everyone. It's exhausting. I just waited for the doctor to come in and visit.

There was never any doubt in my mind that Naesha would pull through. She was under anesthesia for two weeks, and they left her chest cavity open but protected so that she wouldn't get an infection. I had so much to do. Her mom and her sister had the hospital thing covered. My mission was to take care of our child. I didn't have time to be scared, worried, or nervous. I just kept thinking, "You better pull through this, 'cause this boy needs you. You are going to pull through."

I'm not much of a crier, but I cried two times during all of this: when they said what happened, and then when I walked into her open-heart recovery room. She was sitting up and talking, and I was just so amazed that I started crying. When I saw her actually getting back to herself, all I could do was cry. No doubt she was going to pull through, but it was amazing to actually see it. If you aren't a believer after that, there's something wrong with you.

She was in the hospital for a month and out of work for six weeks. When we got home, there were changes—and pills, lots of pills. When she came home, she struggled and had so many restrictions. Not many people consider that they're going to have a very different routine after a life-altering experience. She faced death and beat it. She came home to the same house, but she was different. Looking back, I probably should have gone easier on her about a few things, but it was harder for me to remember that she was different. She was just Naesha. She had been through this huge physical and emotional journey, but I still felt the same. We didn't really register the fact that we weren't coping well. We eventually re-learned to communicate.

Naesha has become really connected to her physical self. If anything is wrong, she goes to the hospital. I think I help to keep her grounded with business as usual. Some days right after, she'd get down on herself, but I'd tell her, "God saved your life for a reason. Not to have a pity party."

She moved on. She got her doctorate. Nothing is going to hold her back. She's energetic, driven, going far in her career, and loves her family. She's doing things now that I always knew she was capable of.

She's always been a diet freak, but we have exercise bikes, and she even got a treadmill for a baby present (I think at her mom's house). She's health conscious, very business oriented, always presentable, makes a great first impression (I love that about her). She always says, "I was doing that before I met you." A lot has stayed the same, but she's really more conscious of her lifestyle. She takes coumadin and beats herself up about missing pills, but she's trying to do the things she needs to so she can live a long life. She takes life much more seriously now, and it's rippled because I know that I could have the same issue. Our family is more conscious of the little things, more appreciative. We say: "Life is not promised so make the most of the one life that you do have."

– Keenan, Naesha's husband

* * *

I remember the days when my heart would beat, and I never knew it was working to keep me alive. Now, I've become keenly aware of every single heartbeat. I can sense my heart contract as it opens and closes to push the necessary blood through my body. This keen sense of awareness has become a part of my here and now. If I listen closely enough, I can even hear my heart speak. There are days that my heart smiles and I consider that smile a gift from God.

I never would have imagined the impact that my situation would have on the people in my life. Strangers, colleagues, family, and churches from all over the world had me on their prayer lists.

There was first grade student in my school who suddenly began to have gruesome headaches. His mother discovered it was a brain tumor. He went from loving every minute of school to never wanting to come to school at all. After months of doctors' visits and trips to specialists, his mother shared that it was in fact a cancerous brain tumor. He had to have the tumor removed. He went in for his very first surgery, and I was fortunate enough to speak to him before the procedure. I told him that I would allow him to use my guardian angel. While we were on the phone, I asked if he could put his hands together so that he would catch her when she left my hands and entered his. He complied. I remember feeling a strong sense of peace and an overwhelming sense of responsibility as well. Somehow, at that moment, I knew my experience would always be a way to strengthen and encourage people regardless of their situation.

You may ask, where was this God you serve when you needed Him? I believe that God never left me, and He was the one that changed the situation that was meant to destroy me into a situation that brought wholeness and deliverance to me and my family. I strongly believe that if you are reading this book with hopes of encouragement or inspiration, God will do the same thing for you in your situation. Believe in your ability to tap into His grace. He will allow you to triumph over your tragedy just He has allowed me to do.

The last five years have been amazing in the sense that I went through a near death experience but was allowed to survive so that I could finish my course in life. I went from never having to take a single pill to a having to take at least fifteen pills a day. I've learned to appreciate the little things in life because it's those things that we can't ever get back once they're gone. To live every day like it's your last, and most importantly, remember that people may not remember every single detail about you and what you've accomplished, but they will always remember how you made them feel. Make them feel worthy of your love.

Over the years, I've been motivated to remain aware of my situation but to use it as a source of strength.

There are times when I want to wallow in self-pity and frustration, but I have to force myself to push through the doubt and emotion and remember that there is much work to be done in my spiritual walk, my family life, and my professional career. My hope is that anyone who reads this book closes it with a sense of urgency to live, and a newfound respect for the power of prayer and the power of our awesome God.

Professionally, my experience has thrown me into the sea of leadership. However, in many ways, I get to use my position to lead by example. Through me, many people had the opportunity to watch God perform a twenty-first century miracle. This process showed individuals how to believe in what's good again.

Staying connected to my source of survival has been the foundation of my success in many areas. I see myself living an abundant healthy life even when my body is telling me differently. I have created a vision of meeting my grandchildren, and I go there in my mind daily. I can see myself doing all these things. If there is a thought that goes against what I believe, I cast it down and think on those things that are pure and of God.

Working to improve damaged relationships and nurturing the relationships that I've already established has been a key part of recovery. This experience has brought me closer to the individuals that I love and has uncovered the existence of people in my life that I didn't love enough.

I've formed extremely close relationships with people who were placed in my path by this experience both in and out of the medical field. They've helped me to understand that God is in the intricate details of our lives, and every connection that is established has a purpose in your life or someone else's. *Before He formed us in our mother's womb, He knew everything about us (Jeremiah 1:5).*

Without the support of my family throughout the entire process, I would not have been able to get up in the morning without feeling sorry for myself—or even find the good in my recovery. There were so many days that I wanted to get in the bed and pull the covers over my head, allowing myself to wallow in self-pity. There were so many days that I felt weak and helpless. Each time I felt my heart skip a beat or when I had to take one of the twenty pills, I was reminded of how vulnerable I really was. Just as I was sinking into a sea of depression, I had my warriors there encamped around me to force me to see the rainbow that often comes after the rain.

Many things happened along my path of recovery, so I searched for ways to push beyond the emotional pain and all the physical aspects and changes that had taken place in my life. Taking the opportunity to shift my focus was key in my recovery. I meditated on the things that I saw myself doing at the end of my recovery. I saw myself being a whole person again.

Being grounded and having a strong faith helped me

to cope with all the adversity. Days when I felt I didn't measure up to anyone's standards, I was comforted in knowing that I measured up to God's standards. Somehow, my faith in Him always led me back to the path of righteousness, which always led me to be victorious. Even the silver lining in my desire to be alone caused me to refer to the words that God left to us all, and that I refer to constantly: *Be strong and of good courage, fear not, nor be afraid of them: for The Lord thy God he it is that doth go with thee; he will not fail thee nor forsake thee. (Deuteronomy 31:6).*

ABOUT THE AUTHOR

Dr. Naesha Parks was born and raised in Thomson, Georgia. She has had a number of spiritual encounters that have contributed to her strong faith and belief that all things are possible to those who believe. Her recent encounter left her with an amazing story that she believes was meant to bless the lives of others. Dr. Parks has ten years of experience in Early Childhood Education and Leadership. She received her Bachelor's degree in Elementary Education and her Specialist and Doctoral degree in Educational Leadership. She is currently serving as an administrator in Columbia County School System. When she is not working on behalf of her students, teachers and community, she spends time with her family. She is married to Keenan and they have four children: Chandler, Sydney, Chance, and Reese.

www.ingramcontent.com/pod-product-compliance
Lightning Source LLC
Chambersburg PA
CBHW020659300426
44112CB00007B/451